Bertha the Beeman

Written by Jill Eggleton
Illustrated by Jim Storey

Every morning,
the Beeman
did the bee dance.

He **clapped**
his hands,
he **slapped**
his knees and
he **buzzed** around
with the buzzing bees.

Buzz, buzz, buzzz!
Buzz, buzz, buzzz!

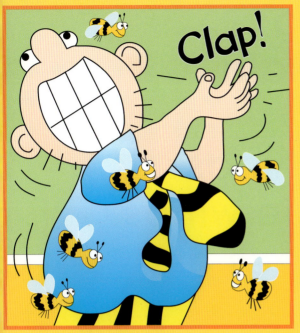

Every morning
the Beeman said,

"Lovely little things
with lovely little wings.
That's what bees are!"

But. . .

Bertha lived next door.
She looked over
the wall and she said,

"**Nasty** little things
with **nasty** little stings.
That's what bees are!"

Every night,
the Beeman
did the bee dance.

He **clapped**
his hands,
he **slapped**
his knees and
he **buzzed** around
with the buzzing bees.

Buzz, buzz, buzzz!
Buzz, buzz, buzzz!

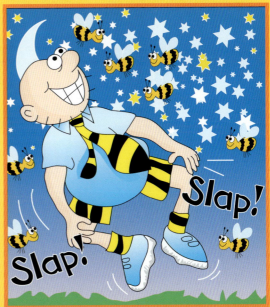

Every night
the Beeman said,

"Lovely little things
with lovely little wings.
That's what bees are!"

But. . .

Bertha looked over the wall and she said,

"**Nasty** little things with **nasty** little stings. That's what bees are!"

One day, Bertha
was painting her house.
She fell off the ladder!
Kerplonk!

The paint fell on her.
Splash!

The ladder fell on her.
Crash!

Bertha was stuck.
"**Help!**" she shouted
"**Help! Help! Help!**"

The bees came buzzing.

Bertha shouted,
"**No! No!**
You are **nasty** little things with **nasty** little stings.
Go away!"

But the bees buzzed around and around Bertha. . .

Buzz, buzz, buzzz!

They buzzed around and around and around. . .

Buzz, buzz, buzzz!

until. . .

. . .the Beeman
came to help.

"Thank you, thank you,"
said Bertha.

But the Beeman said,
"Thank the bees.
Lovely little things
with lovely little wings.
That's what bees are!"

And Bertha said,
"Yes, they are!"

Then Bertha
did the bee dance!

She **clapped**
her hands,
she **slapped**
her knees and
she **buzzed** around
with the buzzing bees.

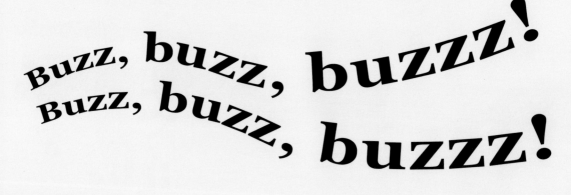

Buzz, buzz, buzzz!
Buzz, buzz, buzzz!

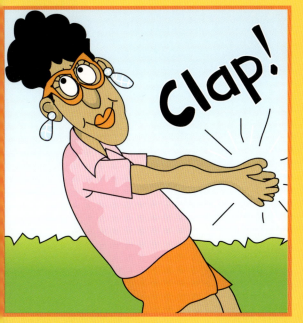

Guide Notes

Title: Bertha and the Beeman
Stage: Year 2

Genre: Fiction
Approach: Shared Reading
Processes: Thinking Critically, Exploring Language, Processing Information
Written and Visual Focus: Change of Text Style, Illustrative text

THINKING CRITICALLY
(sample questions)
- Why do you think the Beeman did a bee dance?
- Why do you think the bees liked the Beeman?
- Why do you think Bertha said the bees were nasty little things?
- Why do you think the Beeman did the bee dance every morning and every night?
- Why do you think the bees went to help Bertha?
- How do you think the bees helped Bertha?
- Do you think this story could be true? Why/Why not?

EXPLORING LANGUAGE

Terminology
Title, cover, illustrations, author, illustrator

Vocabulary
Interest words: buzz, clapped, flapped, slapped, nasty, kerplonk, splash, crash
Contraction: that's

Print Conventions
Capital letter for sentence beginnings and names (**B**ertha, **B**eeman), full stops, exclamation marks, quotation marks, commas, ellipses